Sonnets
of the
Provocative Kind

J.L. Baumann

Printed in The United States of America
Link Printing, Groveland, Florida 34736

No part of this publication may be reproduced in whole or in part, or stored in a retrieval system, or transmitted in any form or by any means, electronic, mechanical, photocopying, recording, or otherwise, without written permission from the publisher. For information regarding permission, write to Post Mortem Publications, 146 East Broad Street, Groveland, FL 34736, or E-Mail:
Contact@Postmortempublications.com

Copyright: ©Post Mortem Publications 2015
All rights reserved

ISBN 978-1-941880-42-5

~ First Edition ~

Experience Divinity

Shakespeare wrote of death and love alike
Spencer scripted godly love in angel form
Ms. Browning surely gave us love's delight
While Frost decided he would not conform

Shelly revealed a mighty King's despair
While Milton brought us virtue to admire
As Keats romanced a joy beyond compare
Byron's shores of freedom wrought desire

Dante Alighieri quested after love divine
Donne epistolized where holiness survives
Millay bore witness as to her pain sublime
Mr. Browning tried to capture death alive

Poets pass away, but their sonnets it is said
Resurrect them every time their poem's read

Table of Contents

Martha	3
A Warm Proposition	5
Capricious Beauty	7
Complete Surrender	9
The Fortunes of Faith	11
E-Inspiration	13
Elizabeth	15
Expose Yourself	17
Fate	19
Graduation	21
Grave Considerations	23
Herald Me a Valentine	25
Homeward Bound	27
A Natural Blessing	29
Just One Look	31
Lovers and Liars	33
The Rewards of Love	35
New Age Thought	37
Nitey Nite	39
Ooh La La	41
A Summer Snapshot	43
Regal Grace	45
Severed	47
Standing Ground	49

Martha

Compassion is thy calling, my Martha come to me
To keep my faith from falling, from my mortality
I need some inspiration, as you can plainly see
So I can understand, the meaning of your poetry

Is it all about your passion, to be the loving one?
To love without abandon, and force me to succumb
To empathy and art, and all that is declared sublime
Like savoring the succulence of grapes upon a vine

In reverent hopes and dreams, I wait for her reply
To have her favors granted, I hope I'm not denied
For within her very nature, and in noble rectitude
She holds the right of clemency in quiet fortitude

And when I often wonder, how she retains her grace
I also pray it's me who put that smile upon her face

A Warm Proposition

Speak not of pleasures past as only memories
They rule the reason why you must proceed
Provoking you to love the smallest of all things
Like sunshine on your face that comes in spring

Appreciate the reason why you age like wine
So drink again, and drink again, until your time
Familiar in the fact, you know the reason why
Your memories give you a purpose to survive

Forget me not, forget me not, they all but cry
When a mother begs another child come alive
Knowing they won't smother other memories
For only new ones help the old ones breathe

So come with me where memories are made
And the sunshine on your face will never fade

Capricious Beauty

Pick me, Pick me, She hoped in desperation
I want to be the one, I want to be the one.
She petitioned and She prayed in wanton declaration
I want to be the one, I want to be the one

Then there were plenty more who prayed
She's not the one, She's not the one
As single mindedly they neighed and all conveyed
She's not the one, She's not the one.

But in finality, and in reality, it was declared
That She had won, Yes, She had won
The crown was Her's and Her's alone to bear
For She had won Yes, She had won.

As heavy is the head that wears the crown might be,
It's still the hand of fickle fate that rules all destiny

Complete Surrender

It is your love that makes me feel alive
Your tender kisses weaken me inside
As I surrender to your soft caress
My heart's forever yours I must confess

You took me by surprise as I gave in
To wanton feelings I had hid within
So now I'm paralyzed and naked too
And all because I fell in love with you

My passion has consumed my very soul
To once again love you, my only goal
So take me now, don't leave me in this way
To not receive the rapture of the day

Your love's a pleasure I can't live without
You are my love and all what I'm about

The Fortunes of Faith

You can't hide from me, the wise old Shaman said
For I am your reality, when I'm inside your head
You think you're all alone, when no one is around
But surely it is known, I can move without a sound

Sometimes I am a twitch, that cannot be explained
Sometimes I am that itch, that drives us all insane
Perchance I am the spirit, that treats you in despair
Perhaps you cannot hear it, but feel that I am there

I'm also there in happiness, escorting your elation
Abating all your sadness, by instilling inspiration
To see beyond the trivial, to all that is worthwhile
And be beyond the physical, the essence of a smile

So dream a dream worth catchin, in quiet solitude
And I'll reward your passion, at our next interlude

E-Inspiration

I'd bought some inspiration, on line the other day
In need of motivation, I'm told it's done this way
I got a colored poster, with someone else's quote
Hoping for some brilliance, a message to promote

When PayPal took my money, inspired by the sale
I gambled that my poster, would soon be in by mail
They guaranteed to send it, as quickly as they could
It had a five star rating, that's what I understood

They noticed me by e-mail, still waiting patiently
Informed me it went e-snail, there was no extra fee
If only they had told me, I'd have paid an extra cost
For without my inspiration, I was desperately lost

So I received my poster, revealing what was said
'A spirit isn't something you can buy upon the web'

Elizabeth

Her hair was raven black, her skin was alabaster
But crimson is her color, you only had to ask her
A single rose she wore, assigned in contradiction
To places felt ignored, for attentive recognition

For placed within her locks, it denoted regal grace
But like the crimson fox, it was never in one place
Sewn on black silk ribbon, secure around her neck
It called to all submission, fore passionate respect

The rose of red professed, surrender to the night
When laid upon her breast, of satin pearly white
I am the queen of hearts, she verily proclaimed
Submit or now depart, for to me it's all the same

But if you stay I warn you, you'll be in my domain
Where a heart of crimson roses, is never ever tame

Expose Yourself

Who are you to read my poem?
Expecting to invade my home
It's sanctity right on display
To catch my soul in disarray

You feed upon the negative
You only take and never give
Integrity you call your own
But never wrote a single poem

Repulsively on love you feast
You hideous demonic priest
And gorge yourself on ridicule
You nasty literary ghoul

I know that I will never see
A critic with a soul to be

Fate

Oh Fate, what do you have in store for me today?
I hope it is amazing and intriguing I do pray
A new and shiny way to make my life worthwhile
As hopefully my destiny will look at me and smile

To rise and meet the unforeseen is all that I can ask
For then to quietly accept, I cannot change the past
For all the days before, you have quietly interned
So I might sanctify the days gone by and learn

That if I want to catch that star, so very far away
In order to achieve it, I must make it through the day
Another dream to witness, I hope you have in store
To give my life excitement, and make me ask for more

So Fate, what have you put on my agenda for today?
For only do I hope it's not the same as yesterday's

Graduation

And so pell-mell they all went into hell
With righteous good intentions
We watched them leave and wished them well
As products of our own invention

So, then we wait, like farmers in the dell
And stay behind, our fates have been decided
We watched them leave, still feeling compelled
To have their needs provided

For now we pause a spell, to listen for the bell
Which tolls for us, awaiting their return
After seeing them leave and bidding farewell
To the very soul of our concerns

But to plant a seed and watch it grow
Is the greatest joy that one can know

Grave Considerations

I sat alone on a fallen tree that lay beside the trail
Do you mind me resting here? I asked to no avail
You surly were a mighty one, I complemented so
But still it did not answer, so I politely did not go

This summer seems a hot one, I testified out loud
When all I heard was solitude, whispering around
I decided it was comfortable, a sitting on that tree
But still this fallen tree, would yet not answer me

Do many come to sit here, I asked that sunny day
To ponder reverently, how it came to be this way
That I should rest upon you, lying on this ground
Accommodating graciously, not uttering a sound

I feel you still can hear me, for spirits do not pass
But when that acorn hit me, it spoke to me at last

Herald Me a Valentine

Cupid, where art thou when I need you most?
Hiding I suppose in heaven's garden of repose
Drinking wine with Bacchus while you boast
O're all the matches you had secretly imposed

Appear to me O' Cupid, Appear to me I say!
For Venus has informed me where you hide!
You can't conceal your whereabouts this day
Your duty bound to act and let you arrows fly

I need a Valentine and surely as it's written
You are the one who consummates this act
Render unto me a sweetheart who is smitten
From your swift and true intentions of attack

And so I must confess, he was a true success
As ecstasy is mine within your sweet caress

Homeward Bound

Into the crowded city I went, to find myself alone
Adventure was my sole intent, a taste of the unknown
I left the mountains' sanctity, born within my soul
To seek out God's humanity, his multitudes extolled

Finally, I had arrived, where nary a tree did stand
For not a single one survived, the cities callous plan
The folks went on efficiently, seeking only pleasure
Praying most deficiently to gold and silver treasure

The mountains' crystal brook was turned into a sewer
And without its natural babble, it had lost all its allure
Vapid was the lightest breeze of jasmine scented air
As animals are tagged and leached in city doctrinaire

Adventures are a curious thing, a mountain of a task
Returning home you realize, you can't escape your past

A Natural Blessing

She is the unexpected rustle of the leaves
She is the witness to the hardwood trees
She is the shadows cast by fleeting birds
She is the calling, speaking not in words

She is the sunshine, bearing love itself
She is the scent that flowers by herself
She is the trickle underneath the brook
She is the necessary time it took to look

She is the earth, the very earth you plow
She is the sky behind the summer cloud
She is the faith that fosters all serenity
She is the grace of mountains' majesty

She is the robin that appears in spring
She is the reason we are blessed to sing

Just One Look

Frilly things that catch my eye do make me smile
Especially, when most attentively, I must surrender
Thoughts I had in mind and lost to this contender
In the flicker of a moment, I could not reconcile
A reason not to look that seemed to me worthwhile
Unashamedly I watched, to be the great defender
A supporter of her show, a witness to her splendor
For most assuredly I testify, the frilly thing had style

Consequences of this act should not be taken lightly
The sight you see can be the cause of your demise
So to tread with caution is the only way to brightly
Discover when intention is the only thing disguised
To lose your independent thought is quite unsightly
But desire trumping intellect, is simply no surprise

Lovers and Liars

There are givers and takers and lovers and liars
And some are the makers of wanton desires
While some are content, to just write the songs
Still others are meant, to just sing along

A composer, conductor, or candy stick maker
A truth telling bastard, or graft ridden faker
Some are the planters, and others the reapers
As some are the kept, and others the keepers

But what is a teacher without any students?
And what is a preacher without any prudence?
Then why have the jailer, without any jail?
And why have a mailman, without any mail?

It's one of life's mysteries, or so I am told
For where there's a pile, there's always a hole

The Rewards
of Love

It's nice to be in love with spring
To find the love in everything
Like feelings never felt before
The joy of youth upon your door

The summer sun bakes in the truth
That love goes on and passes youth
You know that love's the reason why
And pray that it will never die

Fall comes along with certitude
And love's true colors we conclude
Gives brilliance to our lives
And humbly hope as time goes by

When winter comes with its repose
A song of love will be composed

New Age Thought

You notice not the fly before the sex
Its ever presence there had no effect
Before, it's just a speck upon the wall
But after, it's a nuisance, -be it small

You wonder just exactly what it saw
To what conclusion it could ever draw
From a performance held most privately
That wasn't meant for viewing publicly

Then now you think, -a fly can't speak
Of what it saw, in taking just a peek
But then you gasp, well I'll be damned
Perhaps it has a tiny cam!

So swat this thing you now conclude
Before you're featured on the Tube

Nitey Nite

First, it comes as a whisper, carried by the winds of time
Enticingly the great elixir, calls unto thee to be entwined
In cosmic skies enshrined, in heaven's will to be nobility
In all things past or yet to be, embracing infinite capacity

As twilight time evokes an apprehensive contemplation
Vesperically you wonder, beseeching mortal vindication
In the dissipation of the day, surrendering its dominance
In a natural gracious dignity, yielding all preponderance
Patiently you dwell amidst the ambiance of dusky light
And contemplate the vagueness of your nugatory plight
You welcome time to whisk away the clutter all around
To take advantage of the night, to gain insight profound

Then clarity in flecks appear against the pitch black sky
You surrender unto Morpheus and hope to be revived

Ooh La La

There is nothing like a French girl to make a boy a man
Especially in springtime when Chauvin makes his stand
To feel the conquest of desire, within his heart he tries
To find the right selection, a fancy to his eyes

He banters all about the town, to find a medal for his chest
For no way does he want to settle, just for second best
He wonders just exactly, how much it's going to take
To sacrifice naiveté, -his very dignity at stake

He chooses trepidatiously and hopes she won't discover
His undisclosed ineptitude, his weakness as a lover
With charm and femininity, and softness to the touch
Her scent has overcome him, as he surrenders in the clutch

He'll never be the same again, he'll know no greater joy
For there is nothing like a French girl to make a man a boy

A Summer Snapshot

Myrtle, why do you flower before me, outside my window frame
In pink and white and red you wave, as if you seek to be ordained
The more you're pruned, the more you bloom, salaciously in pride
As if you have assumed the right, to now demand I come outside
Perhaps you had no choice, and felt you were compelled to bloom
To demonstrate propitiously that love exists, -explicitly past June
Stark and bright you challenge me, to keep the promises of spring
That in the garden of our youth, we had acknowledged everything

So in my room, in fullest bloom, I got consumed by all her color
Experience my splendor now, she taunted come and be my lover
So, abandoning my window now, I couldn't resist her overt tease
It wasn't hard that summer day to catch her swaying in the breeze
And as the flowered day commenced, I pictured her my lucky fate
Thus when her flowers go to fall, I won't forget this summer date

Regal Grace

I am the show of shows, the thoroughbred had said
For everyone does know, the reason why I'm bred
I'm beautiful to look at, and raced because I'm fast
The people often bet their hats, I'd never finish last

I'm fed the best of oats, and I'm curried every day
I am the toast of all the folks, a magnificent display
I'm trotted out for all to see, myself in all my glory
To justify, most splendidly, an investor's inventory

I know I am expendable, a daily fact I have to face
And it is not contestable, eventually I'll lose a race
So every time I'm harnessed, a victim of my reign
Just like a trophy tarnished, I bear this unashamed

It's said, it is my heart, that makes me run this way
I say I walk up to the start, to only live another day

Severed

I was assigned to stand there, to bear there, wind and rain
I stood there stark and in the dark to mark my place in vain
The wind it blew and through and through, I full well knew
I was the one who had become, the someone who was due

Not a star in the sky to tell me why, I had to make this date
I can't bemoan my creaking bones, alone I knew my fate
In wet regrets and dampened threats and subtitle retribution
I felt the trickle from a bloodless sickle, in final execution

No song was sung while it was done in brutal callousness
Without a simper, or even a whimper, I fell in the abyss
I had become the very next one, to be attritioned and alone
An unknown corpse, a virtual drone, tagged to be disowned

No sympathetic epithets were whirled about in adoration
For it's not a joy to be employed by a giant corporation

Standing Ground

I am the grey that comes from black
The finest marble still has cracks
That light itself intensifies

From shadows deep inside our souls
Our thoughts are forged as black as coal
Escaping, just like fireflies

When hammered hot within your mind
The sparks of knowledge you will find
Fly out before your very eyes

From total darkness into light
In shades of grey you gain insight
From wisdom that before you lies

The bust of Socrates decries
It is ignorance you must defy

Other Publications by J.L. Baumann

Annie Russo - Tenacity Born

Mountain Spirits Speak

A Variety of Passion

A Gothic Rendezvous

Charlie's Country Diner

Farm Fantasies and Figments of Imagination

Mackenzie Goes Adventuring

Chickens Say What?

Chickens Say Que?

www.ingramcontent.com/pod-product-compliance
Lightning Source LLC
Chambersburg PA
CBHW041812040426
42450CB00001B/6